ALSO BY ERIC HORVAT

*Losing Hurts! That's Why Winning Feels So
Good*

Titles written by Eric Horvat may be purchased in bulk for educational purposes, business, fundraising, or sales use. For information, please email ehorvat@directprospect.com.

By reading this, you agree to the following:

You understand this book to be an expression of opinions and not professional advice. You are solely responsible for the use of content and ideas expressed in Get on the Steamroller or Get Run Over. It is recommended for you to do your own independent research before implementing any opinions expressed.

ISBN-13: 978-1470158293

ISBN-10: 1470158299

BISAC: Psychology / Education & Training

Printed in The United States of America

GET ON THE STEAMROLLER
OR
GET RUN OVER

****

THIS BOOK IS DEDICATED TO MY MOTHER, NY, MY
FATHER, PHIL, AND MY BEAUTIFUL WIFE, STACEY

TABLE OF CONTENTS

PREFACE

Let's face it.

If we lived in a perfect world, we would hear something once and we would remember it forever.

I don't live in a perfect world. Do you?

I didn't think so.

"Get on the steamroller or get run over," was spoken to me once by a coach I deeply admire. At the time it felt like an insult.

What it truly turned out to be was a lifelong lesson. I credit that conversation as my inspiration for this book. And this book is a symbol of who I am and what I believe.

I have had the good fortune to meet and play for coaches that I consider great leaders, and I'm very grateful for that.

A light bulb went off in my head and I realized that all of them were very self-demanding. They held themselves accountable. They took responsibility for everything that happened around them. They knew how blessed they were to be in the positions they were in.

They all had similar qualities I admired, and they always pushed themselves and their players to get to their next level. They always pushed to get better, to BE better.

They never settled or were never satisfied with anything they had accomplished. There was always room for improvement.

So if you are reading this, you want to win, or you want to get to your next level.

I have been there. And as I sit here now, typing these words, I am exactly where I want to be. With you.

This should feel different than most books you have read in the past. Right now, you are about to do something a bit different.

We live in a Facebook/Twitter/YouTube/email/text message world now. You will notice that this isn't broken up in a normal paragraph structure. I have chopped it up.

This should give you space to stop and think, or space to write in your own thoughts.

As you go through these pages, come along with me, and take a good look deep inside yourself. Answer the questions asked of you. Answer them honestly. Write them down in the space provided to you. Treat this book like a journal. Take these ideas and concepts, and treat them differently than you normally would.

Let's get to it! We don't have time to mess around!

INTRODUCTION

I went to college, I earned my BA in Psychology and had a great time during those years. I made a ton of lifelong friends, learned a ton of lifelong lessons, and got a good, hard look at winning, losing, success, and failure.

I am going to tell you certain things that I see winners do, how they set up winning strategies, and how they put them into action.

I have a great time talking to athletes about their future, and I love watching people succeed. I am obsessed with the theories tied to success.

I believe winning and success can become infectious…and those are the type of people I want to hang around: winners.

I'm sure most of us think success just tends to happen, like the flu. We don't see it coming, but we know it when we feel it!

That isn't the case, though.

It is not something that is only out there for some of us to enjoy. Greatness and excellence can be found in all of us, and success has many faces.

I truly believe this.

If we have a deep passion in our lives, and we go after it relentlessly, there is no way we can fail. That is what I believe.

And it doesn't need to be any more complicated than that.

Whatever decision you make after reading this, just keep this in mind: Are you living your life with passion, and are you doing something meaningful with it?

I don't know what effect I will have on your life, but I guarantee that if you do everything you read here, and focus on your passion, you will see success and improvement in whatever you are doing.

My parents often told me that I should never carry around the thought "where I am right now is where I am going to be forever." NOW is important, but TOMORROW is more important. So with that thought in mind, I must realize that what I do right now WILL affect tomorrow.

What happened yesterday counts, but need not matter, because you are BECOMING something greater every day. By working hard, you will become better at whatever you do.

And this is probably the most important lesson they taught my brothers and my sister.

The bottom line is this: there are no shortcuts to success.

Most of the successful people we see in our day-to-day lives haven't had lucky situations fall into their laps. They probably weren't handed their success. They didn't get "lucky." They needed to work harder than everyone else at what they were doing. The odds are, the work ethic they had put their competition to shame.

There is no easy way around it. No matter how talented you are, your talents will fail you if you don't have a great work ethic to go along with it.

If you do not work at being better every single day, you will never be able to excel the way you want to. And we all can do more, or push ourselves to do more.

Trust me.

I can remember my mom telling me one time, "Focus on making an impact." And that is what I hope to do one day.

****

The one thing that I see that is noticeably different about athletes who are constantly better than others around them is the attitude they take into what they are doing.

They beat their opponent with their minds (their intellects). They won't let their brains enable failure.

My goal here is to make an impact. My parents made a point of telling me when I was young that if I was going to do something in my life, I should do it to the fullest. And I used to puzzle over this concept as a young boy.

They taught me that if I am going to live here in this country, I need to make a difference. We all have a chance to make an impact. I want my life, my family, and my work to mean something.

We all have success within us. The secret is believing in ourselves. Knowing and believing our potential, and overcoming our limitations.

Do you think your future has already been written, or do you think you have control over what happens?

We all have the power or a choice to either MAKE things

happen or to SIT BACK and let things happen to us. I want YOU to make the choice on WHO you are going to be, WHAT you are going to do, and HOW you are going to do it.

I see it all the time in office settings. Every day, thousands of people walk into their jobs and wait for the work to come to them. They wait for directions from their boss. They are basically passing time Monday-Friday in hopes of a great weekend.

That isn't a goal-driven life. I don't want you to fall into that trap.

Our thoughts, our feelings, and our actions affect the outcome of our lives. If we think of something and commit to something, we are more likely to make it happen.

You CAN do or be what you want if you commit to it.

Don't ever let someone tell you that you can't.

So this is what I want to do. I want to set up a plan for you.

You may know how to do something, but let's figure out how to do the "how-to."

What exactly do I mean by that? It means I want to share with you how you can begin to put yourself in a position to get to your next level.

If you were to ask yourself the question "Have I done EVERYTHING that I am able to do to improve my game?", are you able to answer, "Yes, there is no doubt that I have done EVERYTHING I can to get to the next level"?

I have never met anyone who can say yes with certainty.

Do you want to get to the next level of competition? I'm sure you do.

Here is what I know: most players don't play up to their potential. They play to the level they think they can play, based on what they have done in the past.

If you want to be better, you need to start by having a better image of yourself, and start to do what you already KNOW you need to do, to get to that next level.

In order to do that, it is going to be very demanding. It is going to be very challenging and difficult. It is going to require a lot of work mentally. It is going to require a lot of practice physically. Hopefully, you can push yourself to understand what most players cannot.

It is going to go beyond athletics. It is going to be about how you set your sights for your life. It is going to be about how you set your sights for your future job, and the future relationships you will have with family and friends.

And it will also carry through to the fun you have in life, and how all of this combined together will add up and turn into your life.

Hopefully, as I present some thoughts and concepts about this, it will make sense to you.

I want you to enjoy this, and I want you to find a way to put this into your own game, and use it to put a stamp onto your own life. If there is one thing to take away from all of this, it would be put yourself into a good mindset of not letting one day pass you by without becoming a better athlete.

I used to think I had very little use of my past and everything I had done in my life. I usually wanted not to think about it, and did not take very much time to reflect on how I could use it to help myself in the future.

But I found a way to do this, and hopefully it reveals itself here.

I felt like I never reached my full potential, and I missed out on the next level. I have learned from my mistakes, and I don't want to see others make those same mistakes.

As I began to instruct and do a bit of research on some basic principles most of us follow in life, I noticed two things.

The first thing was that mistakes we make sometimes lead us down a path we didn't intend to take.

The second thing was that successful people, in and out of sports, realize they are given a gift, and they use it. If they can run fast, they get out there and show people. If they can dance, they're the first ones on the floor. If they can sing, everyone hears them sing.

It will all begin with you seeing yourself worthy of getting to the next level. You need to see yourself able to do it in terms of how much effort you put out, in terms of commitment, in terms of ACTION, in terms of preparation, or whatever it is that you need to do to take yourself to the next step.

Look at your life right now, and think of something or someone that is important to you, some person that values what it is that you do.

Now think about some object you would like to have, or some goal you would like to create for yourself, your family, or your team. Now we need to find a way to get to it.

You are going to come up with a plan of action. You are going to make this plan very important. I want it to be something that consumes your mind when you are going to sleep.

You are going to figure out what steps need to be put into place. You are going to take the steps you need to take. You are going to work hard at this plan, and you will be successful at it.

You will, if you BELIEVE you will.

Studying people and watching people has given me a perspective I never want to lose. It is crazy how easy it is to see the good in people, and just as easy to see the bad.

It is incredibly easy to see the bad or the negative in the world.

Television is flooded with negativity. Turn on your local evening news. A feeling of hopelessness comes over me whenever I watch.

The most popular video games are about war, killing, and car theft. The aggressiveness and angst of political and religious debates, work issues, personal relationships, family issues and many other concerning topics are ever-present and contagious.

It puts us in a negative state of mind, and causes a

downward spiral that we may not know how to get out of.

If my day starts out badly, and I allow it to consume me, it does nothing to help me. It only hurts me. And it hurts the people I am around.

It is not uplifting or attractive, and I am not a pleasant person that people want to be around. So I need to be able to "flip a switch" when I feel this way, and turn my attitude around.

We all do.

Think about this for a second: when we turn on the television, a lot of times we are watching other people live out their dreams instead of getting out and living our own dreams.

It's backwards.

We need to be out in the world living our dreams rather than resting at home living through imaginary lives.

And this last point takes us where we are headed: Living up to our dreams, Realizing our hopes, Following our beliefs, and Getting to the next level.

We all want to get to the next level. We have all moved ourselves from one level to the next in some way, shape, or form.

I think we can absolutely do it again and again.

What does it take? Do we need more education than the person next to us? Do we need more money than the person next to us? Do we need to be older and more experienced? Do we need more practice, or more knowledge?

I believe that more than any of these, we need to Believe.

Believe we can get to the next level. Believe it regardless of what anyone else will tell you!

By looking at anyone who has accomplished anything in their life, it is almost obvious that they had a deep sense of belief in what they were setting out to accomplish.

Why is it when we start to think of our goals we will usually set them to a standard that has already been achieved?

Why don't we naturally set our goals so high that they are almost unreachable? Are we afraid of failing?

Are you afraid of failing?

Are your goals set too low? Why are they so low? What are the reasons we have not reached our goals?

Did "stuff" get in the way?

If we think about why we never achieved goals in our lives, it is very likely we will come up with an excuse. We may have what we think is a very good "reason," but no matter what you call the excuse it is still an excuse.

Do our goals change? Absolutely!

But they should change for the good, and become greater, rather than smaller or weaker—or, worse yet, eliminated altogether.

A great coach of mine once told me to change the way I

think about how I approach what I do. Recruiting was tough on me, and because teams say no to you more than they say yes, it can make you feel unwanted.

He asked me, "What would happen if we change the words 'should' be recruited or 'want to' be recruited to 'HAVE TO' get recruited and 'MUST' get recruited?

The whole meaning to the statement changes! Take these examples:

"I should eat healthier" vs. "I MUST eat healthier"

"I hope I play good today" vs. "I MUST play good today"

It adds enthusiasm, passion, and a lot more meaning to the statement. Say it out loud and tell me I am wrong.

I bet you can't.

If you are hearing "I can't" ringing in your ears, then understand that the thing that is talking to you is the little negative voice inside your head. It's your own ego.

It's the same little voice that tells you that you don't look good today. The same voice that tells you, "You are thinking too big."

The same voice that repeats whatever it is that has been holding you back.

Those are internal contradictions and inner battles. That voice inside all of us can keep us from living and fulfilling our dreams.

Back to the idea of sitting in front of the television. What are you watching? Are the people you are watching living their dreams? Did they get "lucky"? Or did they believe they would be where they were?

Change the channel.

Ask the same question about people you see there. Do it again, and again, and again. The people you see have little negative voices in their heads as well, but they didn't listen to them!

They followed their dreams.

They probably failed along the way also. If they didn't fail, they probably didn't learn. Those inner demons, and the little red guy that sits on our shoulders, have kept us down for too many years.

We need to get rid of them!

We all have potential. Most of us don't live up to our potential because we give up too soon. We get discouraged or down on ourselves.

We let other people tell us that the idea we had was bad, or we aren't beautiful, or we don't have the "IT" factor.

Why have we let these people control our entire lives? We need to stop being unenthusiastic, stop acting depressed, perk ourselves up, figure out our dreams, and go after them!

Direct our concentration toward what we want. Take our focus directly where it needs to be. Put our get-up-and-go into what we want most out of life. Apply it to our work, business, faith or religion, family, friendships, and basically every relationship we have.

You see, by applying it…we are doing it!

We are taking action or putting our thoughts into play. If we don't "do," we will not achieve. Nothing is going to fall into your lap. We cannot count on luck. We need a plan. We need to prepare and write out our plan.

Preparation is not something to be taken lightly. Preparation is a big reason why someone is failing or succeeding.

Take preparation into any aspect of life: Work, a speech, a letter, paying bills (you will someday!), etc.

Most of us don't want to be pigeonholed and compare what we have learned in life to sports, or vice versa, but I tend to do it virtually every day.

The coaches who have taught me over the years never received the credit they deserved, and maybe I owe it to them to put what they taught me down on paper.

Oh, and by the way, I will use baseball and baseball-related examples quite often. It was what I played. If you play any other sport, try and compare what I discuss to a specific aspect of your game.

And think about your life. Are you going to get on the steamroller, or will you get run over?

Are you living your life with passion, and are you doing something meaningful with it? What is the meaning of life to you? What are you passionate about and what are you doing to fulfill your passions?

ACCOUNTABILITY

"I am easily satisfied with the very best."—Winston Churchill

What exactly does that mean? Is he never satisfied? Is, "The Very Best," hardly given?

We all aim for excellence, but most of us have a difficult time reaching it.

I interpret this quote as Winston talking about his relentless approach towards everything in his life.

In late 1932, Winston Churchill arranged a meeting with Adolf Hitler before he had come to power in Germany. Churchill wanted to ask Hitler, "How can any man help how he is born?" He was not afraid to call him out on his wicked point of view. Hitler was so angered by the question that he refused to meet with Churchill.

If we look back in history we will see that Churchill was openly against Nazi racism against the Jews in his speeches in the mid to late 30s, even before Britain declared war on Germany. Churchill was the original, modern day human rights activist and ahead of his time. Churchill was criticized for his stance on Hitler. Churchill held Hitler accountable for his views and actions in regard to Jewish people even when many of the leaders in the international community did not.

Holding someone accountable isn't always easy, especially when it's not a popular point of view.

He never settled.

What is "your very best"? Is it always measured in performance? Can it be measured in terms of effort?

There are only two things that are unacceptable to me if I am teaching or coaching you:

> 1. A lack of effort and hustle.
> 2. Blaming other people when things don't go your way.

You don't want to be "That Guy" (or Girl) who is constantly blaming other people when he makes a mistake. Or "That Guy" who never runs out ground balls or walks on and off the field.

We all know this guy. That is the same guy who doesn't work hard when nobody is around but works his tail off when people are watching.

You know those types of players, don't you?

Both lack of effort and lack of hustle are unacceptable because they are IN YOUR CONTROL.

You are in control of how much effort goes into your game. You are in control when it comes time to hustle in between the white lines. You are the person wearing the uniform with your name on the back.

A coach should never have to tell you to hustle. A coach should never have the opportunity to call you lazy.

You had better take pride in the fact a coach never has to worry about you when his back is turned. It is a sign of having self-respect, and respect for the game.

I played on a team where we separated ourselves into small groups and needed to rotate through six stations. We had coaches set up at two or three of the stations, but were on our own for the rest.

When we did not have anybody looking at what we were doing it was our responsibility to put our work in. We had a choice to make, and, of course, a few only put in half the effort they could have, while the others busted their butts to get the exercises completed. Unfortunately, it's in human nature to take it easy.

Fight that urge. What you do when you aren't being watched displays your true character.

Have dignity, and don't be the person getting yelled at for not hustling or getting your work done.

Even worse than not hustling is blaming someone else for a mistake you made or letting the other person be the reason for failure.

Most sports are team games, and no matter the situation you need to find a way to take accountability for the circumstances you are involved in.

Whether, for example, in baseball or softball, it's an at-bat you did not move a runner over, an error in the early part of the game, or a minor miscommunication between you and a teammate, Take responsibility. Put the blame on your own shoulders.

Always be humble. Lead by example.

That's what truly influential athletes do. That's what influential people do.

They take responsibility and step forward when others shy away and step back. You owe it to yourself, and you owe it to your teammates.

****

Every excuse you make keeps you away from the things you want the most in life. Take some time and think about how you can be more accountable in your own life. Who do you blame when things do not go your way? Here's the real question: Who should you hold accountable when things go wrong?

PRACTICE SMARTER

"Luck is a dividend of sweat. The more you sweat, the luckier you get." —Ray Kroc

Greatness isn't handed to anyone, and it involves a lot of demanding work. And even that isn't enough; many people play hard for decades without approaching greatness or even getting slightly better.

What is it, then, that is missing? For most people, sports are hard enough without having to push even harder.

It is about taking those extra steps others don't take. It is about doing what others don't do.

You aren't just doing the task; you're clearly trying to get better at it.

And those extra steps are so difficult and painful they almost never get done.

If greatness was easy, it wouldn't be extraordinary!

Understand that talent doesn't mean intelligence, motivation, or having an outstanding personality.

Nobody is great without work. It takes meaningful, calculated, specific practice.

Simply hitting a bucket of balls over and over is not a smart practice, which is why most hitters don't get better or don't see results more quickly.

Swinging three hundred times with a goal of driving the

ball to all fields, taking good swings each time, continually observing results and making appropriate adjustments, for hours every day—that 's a meaningful practice!

I spoke with one of the smartest players I have ever met about his workout program. As we began to get more in depth about what he was doing, he stopped and took me over to his gear bag.

He opened the bag up and pulled out a notebook. The faded gray cover was bent, the pages were curling, and it was covered in dirt. There was a pen stuffed along the metal binding along the side. I swear this thing was ten years old.

We started sifting through the specifics of what he had been doing offensively, defensively, and in the weight room. It was years of workouts, notes, and advice he had received over the years.

He even had some stuff about the food he eats with a diet plan. It was so specific that it had times of the day and portion sizes written down.

He went above and beyond others.

Now that's a lot to focus on for the benefits of a smarter practice. And it's worthless without one more requirement: do it regularly, not sporadically.

And it's all about how you do what you're already doing. You create the practice in your work, and all it takes is a few critical changes.

And it starts by going at it with a BIG goal: instead of merely trying to get it done, you aim to get better at it.

And you keep your focus where it needs to be: Game speed; all the time!

Have you ever noticed how you can practice perfect, but, when the game comes around, you fail to perform? The ease and relaxed nature of practice disappears, and we tense up and turn into different players.

When this happens, it means we didn't utilize our practice correctly, or we didn't put ourselves in the proper mindset when we were at practice.

We are the same player, right? The ball is the same size, the bat and field are the same, but our brain is different.

Nothing changes but our brain.

We lose trust in our abilities and lose faith in our practice. The sooner you realize and come to terms with this, the faster everything will start to come into place for you.

Maybe we can't expect most players we play with to achieve greatness. It's just too demanding.

But the good news for you is that greatness isn't reserved for a few special or preordained players.

It is ready for you and to everyone who is willing to work harder than you or me.

Feedback is crucial, and getting it should be no problem. But most players don't look for it; they just wait for it, almost hoping it won't come.

If you don't know how successful you are, two things happen:

1. You don't get any better
2. You stop caring.

Frequent feedback needs to be part of your game every day, and every practice. If you aren't lucky enough to get that, then inquire about it, search for it, and seek it out.

****

How are you tracking your progress now? Who is giving you feedback with how you are doing? Are they honest to you? What parts of your game need the most work? How are you going to fix it?

TRY EASIER, WORK HARDER

"The less effort you use, the more powerful you will be."
—Bruce Lee

I didn't play much golf until my early twenties. When I started, I bought a brand new set of clubs and would go straight to the driving range. The first club to come out of the bag was the driver, of course.

Ball after ball I would wack. And it seemed like no matter what I did, the ball would fade away to the right and fall into the safety netting. Had it not been there, the first hole would have been littered with my errant drives.

After a while, an old man came up to me and told me not to hit the ball so hard. He grabbed the club out of my hands and took my place on the green turf.

Nice and easy he went with his backswing, and loosely drove the ball straight down the middle of the driving range.

"You're trying too hard!" he said, "Loosen your grip, and quit hittin' it like a baseball player!"

Guess what happened after that? Every ball started to go straight off the club head. All I needed to do was try easier. Then my hard work in the driving range started to pay off.

(It's funny when a seasoned old vet gives you advice. No matter how happy they may be, the expressions they have always make them look grumpy!)

Nothing holds more value to me as a coach than a good work ethic. Working hard is nice, but there is always someone working harder.

If you took two hundred swings today, someone probably took three hundred. Just when you think you have done enough is the time to do more. Just when you think you can't do any more is the time to dig deep.

Trying isn't what I am talking about when I say "dig deep."

Trying is not enough.

A mentor of mine once said, "A little kid can try, but a champion will find a way to get it done."

I never forgot that after hearing it.

Accomplishing something and reaching a goal you set is digging deep.

When you force yourself to do what is hard, you open yourself up to a realm of results that are untouched by everybody else.

The willingness to do what is difficult is what separates the leaders from the rest of the pack.

It is what champions do, and it is what keeps winners awake at night. Self-discipline and the ability to outwork your opponent are the keys to getting yourself to the next level.

In this world, you will need to do more than just sit back and watch other people get out there and do what it is you need to be doing.

You will need to work your butt off!

If you want to be the person you envision yourself being in the future, work your tail off.

There is no excuse for not pushing yourself to the limit.

Don't just try. Anybody can try. Trying alone will not get you to the next level.

Working hard will.

****

What are some things you can do TODAY to get better? Are you working harder than your competition? What do you think about when your head hits the pillow at night?

STAY CONSISTENT

*"I am not bound to win, but I am bound to be true;
I am not bound to succeed, but am bound to live up to
what light I have."*—Abraham Lincoln

Small tasks completed consistently in a strategic way will create a major impact on your game. Have you ever heard someone tell you that?

In the long run, it's not going to be the big things you have done that will have the major impact. It will be the small things that you did consistently over time.

For example, imagine the things you could get done if you woke up just 30 minutes earlier every single day. Half an hour is not long, but if you multiply those 30 minutes over the course of 365 days, you will give yourself over 7 ½ more days per year.

That is an extra week you will have over your competition!

Throughout your playing career, you are going to do a lot of training. You are going to do a lot of running, throwing, hitting, and strength conditioning.

The more you work out, the better you will be.

Malcolm Gladwell, the famous sociologist, argues in his book *Outliers* that ten thousand hours of hard work is the bedrock to success. Anybody who puts in ten thousand hours or does something ten thousand times is going to be pretty good at what they're doing. Almost an expert!

Consistency is going to be a key to a lot of the success you have. There is a big difference between ten thousand good swings and ten thousand lazy swings.

Always take good swings. Always use good technique when taking batting practice. You must burn the midnight oil with your work ethic.

Promise yourself you will outwork your competition. If you want to be a winner in this life, you've got to follow through on the promises you make to yourself.

When Mickey Mantle was growing up in Oklahoma, every day he would take one hundred swings from the right side of the plate and one hundred swings from the left side of home plate. He later said that little by little he started to see his swings get better, and had it not been for his consistency he would not have been the switch hitter he turned out to be.

Mickey made a promise to himself when he was a child, and followed through on his pledge. Outworking everybody else made him into the man he was. He knew there was always room for improvement, and he never gave up on himself.

In order to reach and attain your goals, you are going to need to be responsible for your own consistency.

You have got to be accountable!!!

A coach can check on you, your trainer can push you, but ultimately, the job belongs to you.

Be relentless in your approach, set the expectations high, and exceed your objectives. It is what you are doing on the other side of the wall, when nobody is watching, that determines your character.

****

If you were to be judged based on what you have done when nobody is looking, how would you be rated? What are some specific things you can do to improve this?

IDENTIFY & IMPROVE YOUR WEAKNESSES

"All the adversity I've had in my life, all my troubles have strengthened me...You may not realize it when it happens, but a kick in the teeth may be the best thing in the world for you." —Walt Disney

I don't care how good you think you are, you have some weaknesses. Denying that you have them, and failing to develop the skills related to them, will limit your overall value, or worse yet, end your career.

If you don't recognize a problem, you will never take the action to fix it.

Let's put a spin on this: a weakness is not necessarily negative; it's just an indication of strengths you'll need to work on to get to your next level. Yes, this is optimistic, but it's true.

Identifying your weaknesses can prove to be one of your strengths in your mental game. It shows that you can have an objective view of your game, and it will help you determine new weaknesses as your performance evolves with each new level you reach.

Recognizing your own weaknesses is vital.

Asking others what your weaknesses are is also important. The two may not always align, or it may not be what you want to hear.

But remember this: if one person can see it, others can as well.

Put in time, focus and energy to progress and better enhance your all-around abilities.

Your personal development will depend on it.

****

What is your biggest weakness? What tasks are you going to do to improve them? If you work hard enough at them, do you BELIEVE you can turn them into strengths?

LOVE YOUR STRENGTHS

Your strengths and unique abilities are your most precious assets.

I want you to look back on your career. What have you accomplished? Were you or are you the standout player in your league? Did your stats show how good a player you are? How do other people describe you? Are you the type of player a coach always wants on his team?

Everything that makes you proud of yourself is a strength.

These strengths should empower you and supply you with confidence.

They should make you walk around with your head held high. They should let you feel whatever it is you need to feel in order to be at your best.

That is because THIS is you when you are at your best.

I know that I feel my best when I know I worked myself to the point of exhaustion. When I have pushed myself to a certain limit. I know I pushed myself to be a better person and pushed my body to be better than it was before the workout.

I sleep better, I'm in a better mood, and I feel confident.

Write out what your strong suits are.

Refer to this list when you feel like you are in a rut. You need to remind yourself of the great qualities you possess.

Use these hints to keep your mind where it needs to be and to help keep your focus. Keep this list and add to it from time to time.

Don't ever lose it. You will appreciate it more and more the older you get.

Know that you are valued on your team and that you will be valued in the future. Know that you will carry forward everything you are good at and utilize your skills and strengths for new games and situations and on different teams.

Write your strengths in here, and come back to the list whenever you experience times of weakness and doubt. Come back here when you need to remind yourself of who you are and who you intend to be.

WRITE YOUR GOALS DOWN

I know you have goals for your future. I know you do, because all players do. They can be as simple as making the squad or as big as making the pros.

It does not matter how big or how small, write them down on paper.

Make it a habit, and update them regularly.

Why should you do this? Why is it important?

By writing your goals and ambitions down, you are creating a "contract" with yourself. This also can spark new motivations you never knew existed and make you much more likely to achieve them.

Post them somewhere so you will see and read them often.

This will motivate you to get to the next level.

Add to your goals. Edit them as time passes.

Be realistic, though.

You do not want to over-exaggerate or write down something that is unattainable. In light of the notion that BELIEF matters most, what counts as unattainable? How will you distinguish something that's truly unattainable from something that is very difficult or distant? What are the consequences of aiming too high?

Also, jot down how you will achieve these goals, and set

a date for when you want to complete them.

University studies have shown that a high percentage of those who wrote down their goals were able to achieve them within twenty years.

Why shouldn't it work for you, as well?

If you don't know where to start, here are 6 points that will get you going (WRITE THEM DOWN!):

1. Where specifically do you want to go, and/or who do you want to be?

2. Exactly what are you going to do to get where you want to go, or be who you want to be?

3. Write down a date when you will start.

4. Write out or create a plan, and put it into immediate action.

5. Put 1-4 all together to further clarify your specific goal

6. Read what you wrote above once in the a.m. and once in the p.m.

Another way to help solidify and realize your goals is to share them with someone you love and trust.

Instead of sharing your frustration and unfulfilled goals in a negative way, which will only bring others down, share a goal that you deeply aspire to, and you will be strengthening your own character, as well as the people or person you are speaking with.

In a way, telling someone you trust what your goals are lessens the feeling of not having reached the goals.

When you share it openly, it reinforces that you want to accomplish it.

The same concept we spoke about in writing it down is done here as well.

In applying these strategies, we are separating complaining and sharing.

Everyone hates complainers. We don't want to listen to them, and if you know one, you probably tune them out.

However, sometimes it is fun to hear what others have going on, as far as goals are concerned. Think about how you would react to the following two statements about practice.

"I hate practicing. It sucks! We always do the same thing."

vs.

"Do you know what I would really like to be doing in practice?"

In the first sentence, you are complaining about something you have to do. In the second sentence, you are setting yourself up for success in a positive manner.

How would you react if someone said these statements to you?

In the first case, you would want to get away or go hang out with someone else. In the second, you would want to hear more. You would want to actually connect or engage in a conversation with that person.

Telling someone your goals is also a great way to clarify what you really want, and realize what you may not actually be able to become or achieve.

Spend some time reflecting on your goals.

Think of your complaints and turn them into positive expressions. You may find that those closest to you want to hear all of your goals and a lot of what you have to say.

I want your goals to come true, but even if they don't all come true, I hope you still share them with others, along with writing them down.

PAST PERFORMANCE

Most players are given labels.

We all label ourselves, as well.

Pull hitter, power hitter, defensive specialist, etc.

What is your label? Becoming a more well-rounded athlete should be a goal for all players.

Everything we have done is usually recorded. In baseball and softball, we take pride in the fact that we can compare each other based on numbers.

And those numbers never lie. If you led the team in RBIs, you were a valuable hitter. You produced for the team.

If you stole a lot of bases, you took liberties away from the other team. You limited double plays. You minimized the middle infielders' range.

Being categorized only makes scouting reports on you easier to create. But at the same time, they can allow you to strike fear in your opponents' eyes.

Do not fear what other people or coaches think.

Be comfortable taking risks with working on different parts of your game. Explore your weaknesses in order to put together or formulate a plan that eliminates a stereotype or label that has been placed on you.

If an opposing coach brands you as a pull hitter, he most likely will put a "shift" in the defense in order to capitalize on your label.

Recognize how you are typecast, and utilize this to your advantage. Know how your opponent will play you and think ahead. Beat them at their own game.

Don't allow past performance to be the breakdown in an at-bat. Understand how you will be pitched, identify what is happening, and get the most out of knowing the expectations others have placed upon you.

YOUR BRAIN WILL CONTRL YOUR BODY

Your brain is in control. You are tougher than you think.

The negative feelings, which all of us can feel when playing our sports, are the reasons we fail. They are the reasons we do not get ourselves to the next level.

Those feelings are fear crawling into your brain.

They are fears we learn. Where did we learn these fears?

Was it our parents? Was it from our friendships? From teammates?

We need to eliminate these fears. We need to convince ourselves that we do not fear anything. We need to be ready.

Are you ready?

Have you established your own good habits? Have you determined your desires and your passions in life?

What processes have you put into place?

The answers to these questions lie in your own mind. It is in your brain. It is in your soul. It is in your heart.

The answers have been within you the entire time, your entire life, but you did not know it. You have seen people believe in you.

Poor decisions have been made, and great decisions have

been made.

All of these decisions started in your own brain, and were shaped by your emotional state at the time of making the decisions.

I have found ways to take bad situations and make them good. I have also been in bad situations and not turned them into something good.

I have made tons of mistakes.

I have learned from my mistakes, I have developed good and bad habits, and all along I have had control without knowing it.

Knowing it is all the difference. Your brain will control your body.

Make the right decisions. Be prepared.

Work harder than the other person. Take every inch you can, and bend it to work for you.

Your brain must do it before you body will.

Mastering your brain is learning how to take control of your life. It is learning how to channel your energy deep within yourself so that you can deal with whatever life happens to send in your direction.

It means checking within you on the inside, not the outside, for significance, recognition, and progress.

Controlling your brain is learning to accept those situations you cannot change, and changing the situations you can.

REVOLUTIONIZE YOUR GAME

Taking care of yourself, inside and out, is essential for building the confidence you need to lead. Whether you are at home, at practice, or in a game, you want your strength and performance from everything you have learned, to power your success.

Your game plan needs to involve smart strategies that force you to learn from mistakes, because you are definitely going to make them.

Life is hard enough. The many demands of school, sports, family life, friendships, and everything else that obligates us are hard to keep up with.

Tell yourself you are going to commit to breaking your bad habits and revolutionizing yourself for your own good.

You know what you do wrong, and change is very hard.

You need to know that choosing determination over lethargy, discipline over laziness, and self-sufficiency over pity is what will get you to the next level.

It is very difficult, and 99% of the time we fail to make the proper changes.

It involves letting go of the past and freeing yourself of the habits you have developed over years. Habits you were taught as a kid. Techniques that hurt more than help.

Not changing is easy. Changing requires work.

Knowing what you need to do is the first step.

Committing to what you need to do is step number two.

Deciding and acting upon the commitment is the third step.

This will eliminate any bad routines, and reflect that you know that it is worth the effort.

The road is long, the road is bumpy, but the outcome from your commitment will teach you life lessons and pay off in the long run.

It will be life-altering.

When life is hardest you must narrow your focus and keep going. Push to revolutionize your game.

HOW YOU THINK IMPACTS WHAT YOU DO

What is better for you after a practice? A can of Coke, or a bottle of water?

The answer is simple, right?

Anybody can answer that question. A child can confidently answer that question.

But people still make the wrong decision, don't they? People still go for the Coke, knowing it is the wrong decision. People still choose the Coke, or the bag of chips, or the candy bar and make a bad choice on a routine basis.

Small choices like that are what are going to separate a winner from the loser.

It isn't anything innovative.

We all know that the choices we make—between water and Coke, practicing and not practicing, watching TV and studying—are going to impact our future.

One is good for you, and one is bad for you. One will allow you to hydrate, sleep better, improve muscle development, and so on.

The other will not.

Hitting, running, throwing, stretching, eating properly, and working at the gym are all things that are going to make you a better athlete.

We know right from wrong.

The key is understanding why we should do the right thing.

You are in a position right now to make the right decisions. You are in a position to do the little things. You are in a position to do the little details that will make you a better athlete.

By reading this right now, you are putting yourself in a position to get better.

Success needs to sustain itself with more success.

You must build on top of your accomplishments. If you went four for four last game, what does that mean for today's game? How well does that work for you in the game today?

It means nothing.

Each day, each game, you must start over.

Success is never-ending.

The "what have you done for me lately?" idea is 100% correct in this situation.

Don't live in the rearview mirror. Don't live in the past.

Focus on today, and focus on the future.

Don't dwell on negativity. Do you agree?

WHAT IT TAKES TO BE GREAT NEVER CHANGES

You can only think about one thing at a time.

When you think about distractions and all kinds of other things going on in your life when you are supposed to be hitting, throwing, or working out, you are diverting from your goals.

One of the things it takes to be a great athlete is recognizing when you are distracted.

Recognize that you are going to become unfocused at times, and snap out of it. Refocus!

Being great and the philosophies about being great have never changed.

Hard work...determination...fortitude...You pick the noun that best describes it. There are hundreds of them.

The great players in history had them all.

Think about the way that you talk to yourself in your head. Think about how you communicate with yourself.

That inner voice is what will lead you down the path to success.

Recognize the traits that some people have that could hinder your ability to be successful: not being on time, sleeping too much, missing class, coming up with excuses, not taking enough swings or getting enough reps, being more concerned with "style" or "looks" than with your "core."

Do you recognize the theme here?

Winners got to the top because they focused on doing the right thing.

They earned the right to be called great.

And they stayed great because they built on top of early success day in and day out.

You have an opportunity right now.

You will have an opportunity in the next hour. You will have an opportunity tomorrow. You will have an opportunity this season. You will have an opportunity next season.

Identify that you have the ability to capitalize on opportunities every second of every day.

Don't waste them.

Benefit from these opportunities by keeping your mind on the simple things.

It is no different than going shopping at Ralphs.

If you go to the grocery store without a list, you might buy the wrong things.

You have to go into practice with the mentality, "This is what I am here for today."

Great opportunities are out there for you to have. Get excited about them. Get excited about getting better.

You have the chance to do it.

Do you think you can get better? You had better. Your last at-bat or your last pitch did not define anything for you.

It was a starting point.

It was something to build on. You are going to get better. You are going to raise your expectations, and you are going to do what it takes to get to the next level. You are going to keep moving forward.

You need to know it, and you need to live it.

LEARN FROM OTHERS MISTAKES

Say we have a goal. What strategy do we put into play to achieve it? Why not look to other people who achieved those goals and study what they did?

History repeats itself, right?

Well then, let's learn from other people. Learn from other people's mistakes. Learn from other people's successes.

Let's take advantage of the knowledge we are given from others.

Successful people have similar habits. Some of the habits are visible from the outside, but most are mental.

Some of the most successful athletes and business men didn't come from the best universities and cities in the world. But what they had was an unbelievably strong mental mindset.

A mental mindset—a strong and wide sense of awareness—heightens your enthusiasm and, most importantly, the belief that you will be successful.

Past winners believes they would be successful more than they believed anything else in this world.

Their mental mindset was stronger than everyone else's, and they prevailed.

How mentally tough are you?

AIM TO BE THE BEST IN THE WORLD!

Why can't we be the best in the world at something? Is that too big of a goal?

Why can't we shoot to be the best in the world at something? Are we fed so much negative influence that we quit? Are we dejected so much that we abandon our dreams?

It is possible; we just need to find what it is we want to be the best at, and challenge ourselves to make that happen.

If you don't believe it is possible, then it isn't.

We hit adulthood and our dreams get smaller and smaller. We still set goals and dreams.

But the dreams get more and more attainable.

The goals and dreams are so small we don't have any problem reaching them.

We do what we do because of Motivation or Inspiration. Each of us needs to ask ourselves which of the two has generated our behavior.

If we have bigger goals than everyone else, how do we remain inspired?

The answer is to do what you love.

The more successful you are, the more likely it is that you

will move into a position that will take you away from doing the things that you are good at and that you like to do.

You take on more accountability and responsibilities, so as a result you will have less time doing what you care about and what you are concerned about.

Resist that current. Do what you love.

Learn from what is happening to you in each game. You are going to miss out on a lot of improvement if you don't take the time to check up on yourself regularly.

Getting caught up in the day-to-day tasks of practice makes it easy to forget your dream of the future. As a consequence of that, you may not aim high enough, or far enough.

It is easy to spend too much time feeling like a victim, rather than asking, "What am I going to do to make it better?"

Mirror people who are successful around you. Find role models worthy of your attention.

Find someone who plays the game in a manner in which you want to play, or someone who has made an impact on you and others.

Strong challenges are commonly connected with strong results.

Sure, you can get lucky every once in a while and find an easy path to success. But will you be able to sustain that success, or is it just a fluke?

Will you be able to repeat it?

If we set up a small goal and reach it, are we hitting our full potential?

We know the answer to that question. What are you going to do about it?

YOU ARE HARD-WIRED TO WIN

A human being is hard-wired to grow and be successful.

Our brain is born with habits we do not have to learn.

Those are called instincts.

They have been imprinted into our being, and when competing in a game or facing a challenge, we can see that we are hard-wired to want to win.

A human being is hard-wired to thrive. If we were not, we would still be roaming around the planet in buffalo skin grunting to each other to communicate.

We are hard-wired to win. Every moment in our lives will affect the next moment.

If you do not believe this, look back on your life and think of how you could have made a different decision.

What if you had decided not to take the job? What if you had decided to move to a different city? Take a major event in your life—any event—and remove it from your past. Where would you be? Who would you have met? Who would you NOT have met? What would NOT have happened?

We are hard-wired to win.

When you put in big work, you will get big rewards. When you throw your heart and your desire into your practice, you are going to get big rewards back.

Big effort brings big rewards.

If you look throughout time and at the greatest ballplayers, you will see over and over again that those players put major work into improving their craft. It was practically imbedded into their consciousness.

Your mind is the key to your success or your failure.

DO YOU SETTLE FOR LESS?

Should we settle for less than what we are destined to be?
Should we settle for less than what we are destined to do?
Should we settle for less than what we are destined to
create?

Never.

We should direct our mind and our casual thoughts
towards helping and understanding as many people as
possible. Then using what we learn to become better
athletes.

I am sure you have plenty of abilities and skills. But the
question you need to be asking yourself is:

"How much talent do I have, and how much of it am I
failing to utilize on a daily basis?"

We should try to help as many people as possible. We
should try to better as many lives as possible. We should
do whatever it takes to use our potential to improve the
mental or physical health or other people and improve
people's lives forever.

But unfortunately, we all give that up.

We give it up because of responsibilities.

We give it up because society says, "it's time to settle
down."

We give up because we follow other people's lead. But
the people we are following are the wrong people to

follow.

Never use your circumstances as an excuse to give up on your dreams.

Do not settle for less than what you think you are worth.

WHERE DO YOU GET YOUR ADVICE?

Unfortunately, we ask the wrong people for advice.

We take advice from people who give it to us without our asking. We should be asking for advice from someone who has done it before.

From someone who has done it successfully before. Someone who has accomplished the goal you are reaching for.

Successful people are willing to do what others are not.

We have heard that many times in our lives but have not followed through on it. It is sound advice, but we have all lost our way.

Someone who has done it before did not quit in the early stages because they did not get any immediate gratification. They took full advantage of their physical and mental strengths, and looked past the short-term gains and focused on the long-term results.

Their passage through their success may have seemed long and unmarked by any unusual or important occurrence, but once they got to the top, they were able to describe the journey by combining all the individual parts and constructing a detailed description of how to succeed.

And they HAVE succeeded!

STAY STRONG, STAY POSITIVE

If we have a choice of many restaurants in our city to eat at, do we want to choose the second-rate restaurant? If we choose to go on a vacation, do we want to choose a middle-of-the-road vacation spot?

Then why do we choose a mediocre life?

Most people on this planet are mediocre. We don't want to be mediocre, we want to be great.

We want to be the best in the world at something.

Life is a voyage, and it is full of trials and tribulations along the way. It is how we handle these challenges that will determine how successful we are.

And when talking about success, it is not as important WHAT we are doing to be successful as it is HOW we are doing it to be successful.

How are we practicing? How hard are we practicing?

We need to be capitalizing on our potential. The odds are, you are not doing this.

What percentage of your day is spent towards capitalizing on your potential? One hour? Two hours? Less than that?

You say you want to be better. You say you want to get to the next level.

How many days off in the week do you take?

If you are unable to achieve or reach a certain goal, what exactly is it that is holding you back? How come others around you are able to do it, but for some reason you can't?

Why do you fall in the middle?

Take a look deep inside yourself. Think about how much extra you do.

Right now, you should either be extremely proud of yourself and all the work you do, or you'd better be embarrassed at how much more you really could be doing to improve yourself.

When you look at someone who is successful, we tend to look at what they have done and label it as their talent.

"Wow, little Johnny is such a talented ballplayer!"

We don't look at as the result of many, many hours of hard work. We don't say, "I bet Johnny practices a lot harder and a lot longer than everyone else on the team."

We sometimes look at it as an "innate" ability. This is the wrong way to look at it. Instead, when we see success we should think about how much hard work it took to get there.

How many hours in the gym were put in? How many extra swings did he take when the coach wasn't looking? How many extra ground balls did he field? What kind of burning desire did he have that pushed him to outwork everyone else?

That person did not settle to be mediocre.

They did not take the easy way out.

They pushed themselves when nobody told them to push.

There are millions of areas in which we can be successful—business, family, friendships—and there are varying degrees of success in each one.

How you approach each will determine your success. So, again, it is not WHAT you are doing, but HOW.

If we follow this approach, we will see positive results from our actions, and big results are what we are looking for.

WE ALL HAVE 24 HOURS IN A DAY

We don't have enough time to reach our goals. Isn't that an excuse you hear a lot?

"I don't have enough time."

We don't have enough time to do the things we want to do in life because life gets in the way.

This is a negative way of dealing with our shortcomings. We all know we have twenty-four hours in a day.

Some people are able to accomplish more. Why?

Their plan is sharper.

Their attack is more direct. They know what they are going to do before they do it.

They have time because their direction is pinpointed at what they want.

They have time because they MAKE time.

It was more important to them than it was to everyone else!

That is a winner's attitude. A good attitude plus a good way of thinking about what you are doing will provide you with success. Do a little, a lot. Not a lot, a little.

Put your efforts in bit by bit to create something great, rather than putting everything together all at once to create something great.

Your desire, resolve, and relentlessness will provide you with the results you want. Be a leader, not a follower.

Be relentless.

SURROUND YOURSELF WITH SUCCESSFUL PEOPLE

We all know we have potential. Most people know they are full of potential. Most people don't reach their full potential.

Most people don't go out and grab what it is they are looking for.

A majority of people allow the negative people or the "realists" to tell them it cannot be done.

A "realist" will take the negative experiences of their own lives and assume they will happen to you.

They have, in a sense, given up on their dreams and their belief of the "good" that is naturally inherent in people.

Goodness or wholesomeness is natural for a human being. Just look at a baby or a toddler, before it has experienced some form of negativity from a parent.

Their world comes crashing down near the age of one or two because of the negativity shown to them by the parent.

Negative people will always say they are "not negative, they are realists." The "reality" they speak of are past negative experiences they have not been able to overcome.

The only reality these people are talking about is the reality in their own mind.

They have already told themselves the world is a bad place. They have already told themselves the government is corrupt. They have already told themselves they will never make enough money.

Don't let them suck your dreams away from you.

Don't let them suck your beliefs away from you. Don't let them bring you down with them.

Surround yourself with good, smart, successful people.

****

Who are you around and whom do you talk to every day? If you could talk to anyone in the world, who would it be? How would they change your life?

SOMEONE ELSE HAS DONE IT BEFORE YOU

There have been billions and billions of people who have lived on this planet for tens of thousands of years. No matter what you are going through or what you are feeling, someone else has felt or gone through the same thing.

Your problem or whatever is holding you back is nothing new.

Someone else has done it and lived it.

Learn from the billions of people who have lived life. Learn from them by studying them.

Study their mistakes, but more importantly, study their good habits.

Study the traits that made them successful. Study their personality and what made those people winners.

What was their objective? What were their goals? How much effort did they put into reaching those goals? How much time did they spend focusing on those goals?

Did they take organize their thoughts and their actions in an effort to reach their objective? Did they act on their instincts and take some form of action to get there?

Did they get off their thinking chair and take action on their thoughts and ideas?

What did they do?

How strong was their belief system? How strongly did they believe they could be successful? How resilient was their faith in themselves?

Were they productive?

Did they get better and better at what they were doing as time when on? Did they reach more and more people with their message or their creation? Was all their energy going into reaching their goal?

Ask the questions above about any historic figure throughout time or about any successful person you may know or emulate, and see how your answers follow a similar pattern. These are the steps we all must take to accomplish anything.

It can range from getting up in the morning and cooking eggs to becoming the president of your company.

But if the little man on your shoulder tells you "you can't do it" and you believe the voice…well, that is just enough doubt to allow you to fail.

****

Where do you want to go or who do you want to be? Who has done what you want to do? Are you doing what successful athletes before you have done?

FOCUS ON THE DREAM

People want to be helped. People want to help themselves.

But the question is, do people know how to help themselves? "If only I had a million dollars, then everything would be fine."

But would it?

What original problems caused the need for the million dollars? Were there financial mistakes? Was money lent to the wrong people?

Can you take accountability for all of the problems you are facing in your life? Do you blame other people for your problems?

There is always a way to take accountability for your mistakes and troubles you have faced and will face in the future. Is the traffic something you can control? Can you control unbelievably long lines at the airport?

What do you want to represent? Do you want people to remember you?

How do you want people to remember you? What do you want people to remember you by? What are you going to do to make an impact so that people remember you?

Do you believe you have something special about you that will make people remember you? Do you do more for others, or do you expect others to do more for you? Do you have the energy to do something memorable?

Will this memory be a lasting memory? Will it be a quick memory for people? Will it give you a legacy to leave behind?

Answer all of these questions as you read them. Pause and THINK. We all have something deep down in us. Some drive, some determination, some purpose in life.

Find your purpose in your athletic dream. Focus on it and ask yourself, "Am I doing everything I can in order to reach my dream?" If you answer this question with a "NO" then it is time to get to work.

It is time to take some action.

It is time to motivate yourself rather than wait for someone else to motivate you.

GO THROUG EACH DAY WITH A PLAN

Going through your career without a solid plan is like eating soup with a fork.

It looks like it might work, and you can see the soup splashing around and moving, but you are making no forward progress.

It's all going to come down to practice. Whether you know it or not, you are practicing.

You are one of the rare people in this world at this time and in this place. Do you want to be a person who will step up and be a leader? Do you want to produce? Are you a producer?

Do you focus?

Your desires must come from within. What you are thinking about is what will cause an emotional reaction inside you.

If you have goals but believe you're a loser, no matter how hard you struggle you will not be able to achieve your goals.

Something will always bring about a reason or an excuse that will cause you to fail before you get close to it.

Do you want to know how to create the perfect life? Do you want to get to the next level?

Of course you do. Observe the people around you, and

understand that they have all created their own destinies.

This game of life is supposed to be fun. Do you agree? We do not need to fixate our thoughts on our negative desires.

We do need to fixate, though. We need to fixate on what we desire most in this life and in our sport.

We need to revolve our lives around this fixation. This fixation needs to be so strong in our minds that nobody or nothing can get in our way. It needs to become our destiny. What is your destiny?

Think about it.

What can you picture in your mind right now? What emotions are you feeling?

What is around you? Who is around you?

Put this image in your brain, and visualize what you want.

GET THERE 15 MINUTES EARLY

When you over prepare yourself in practice, you give yourself the advantage to not tense up or worry because you are geared up and ready to go.

It is easy to underestimate preparation.

It would do us well to over prepare. And you would be doing yourself a huge favor if you showed up fifteen to thirty minutes early to wherever you are going.

I feel being on time means being fifteen minutes early. I was always taught that it is better to be ahead of schedule and wait than to have others have to wait on you.

I harp on this all the time and I think it will serve you well.

You won't go into games tense because you were there early, prepared for the game. It lessens the anxiety.

Throwing things together at the last minute and rushing to the field isn't going to lead to a good game.

Being routinely late has many disconcerting effects on you and others around you.

If you are late all the time, you miss out on a lot of things. If you show up for a meal when dessert is being served, you missed the meal.

You eat cold leftovers. If you show up at halftime to a football game, you miss most of a great game.

Being on time is a matter of priorities.

It also affects your reputation. If you are always late, your reliability and commitment are questioned.

If you can't even be trusted to be on time, others will not be able to depend on you for other things. How can I depend on you to hit a double in the gap if I can't trust you to be where I need you on time?

It may also cause bitterness from others, because they feel you do not put an importance on getting to the field time with them. You are showing that you feel your time is more important than theirs.

Being late does not only affect you, but also everyone around you.

Get to the field early.

VISUALIZATION

What are we capable of? Do the talented always win over the un-talented?

Do the people with more education always win in life?

If we don't have the same proficiencies as the other person, are we destined to fail?

We are capable of more than we think. Our beliefs can bring us to levels we never knew existed.

Having a positive mindset can push us to an intensity we won't even recognize.

If we never did the things we dreamed, of we would still be cavemen. If we never fell as infants, we never would have learned to walk without falling.

What visions do you have? How often do you have these visions?

Picture yourself hitting the ball, running with all your might, and record how that makes you feel. Bring those images and feelings with you when you step on the field. It will make a huge difference.

Are these visions so powerful that you believe they will come true?

CHANGE IS NOT THE ENEMY

It is very normal for people to fear change. It brings us out of our comfort zones.

Change is unavoidable.

We cannot see it as our enemy. The important part is controlling what we are going to change, putting a process in place, and following that process to achieve our goal.

We sometimes think that the larger the change we are trying to make, the longer, and harder, and more difficult the progression of the change is going to be.

This is our first reaction when we are told we need to change. But this is not the way it has to be. We need to look at change differently, and take the challenge head on.

We must be aggressive in our approach and fearless with our attitude, and we must move toward the challenge with a relentless mindset.

Avoid having too much resistance to changes; you will need to view them as adjustments that should be considered self-improvement. You can manage yourself, and positives will come about if you are ready.

Put a strategy into play. Have a plan set out as to what steps you will take to make the necessary changes.

Have a clear message in your mind as to what you are going to modify. Solve problems throughout the process.

For example, in baseball or softball, change means

moving your feet in your stance, modifying the way you run, raising or lowering your arms in your batting stance, your arm slot if you are a pitcher, or even reconfiguring your overall training program.

Understand that change is necessary in order to get yourself to the next level.

Even high performance vehicles need a tune-up from time to time!

Monitor your progress when making your adjustments. Make a list, just like goal setting.

Work on them daily, and be tough on yourself. Making things easy will never lead to a successful change.

TAKE YOUR PARENTS' ADVICE

The people who probably know you as well as anybody in the world are sometimes the people we often take for granted, and those people are your parents.

Why do I say we take our parents for granted?

There are a lot of reasons.

Maybe we don't take them seriously. Or as we get older we pick apart their flaws. Or as we become more educated we don't think they know us like they used to. Maybe we think they don't know us inside and out.

But the truth of the matter is, they do.

People are often the same person they were when they were a kid running around in the living room and playing ball in the house.

People are the same because their heart is the same. Their "soul" is the same.

Our parents can see our quirks and our weaknesses, and they can see how we can be our own worst enemies.

Your parents are likely to be twice your age, and will have been through their own tough times as they have raised you, as well as the tough times you have experienced. They faced those, as well.

Remember this: it is much easier to give advice than it is to listen to it.

It is easier for others to see how we can better ourselves than it is to see it ourselves.

Ask for advice from your parents. They will not lead you in the wrong direction.

Love your parents, and learn from them. Parents never stop being parents, no matter what age you are.

Use their wisdom.

PRACTICE! EVEN WHEN YOU DON'T FEEL LIKE IT

Great ballplayers accept that they can't control everything around them. They know that giving up full control is one of the best ways to gain command over the chaos surrounding them.

For example, if you wake up in the middle of the night, know that accepting sleeplessness is the best way to fall back asleep.

You need to accept that almost every choice in life is a choice between sacrifice and compromise. If you practice and push through, even when you don't feel like it, you will face a future with results that will speak for themselves.

Something shared by all the good ballplayers I have known was the ability to get themselves to practice, regardless of how they felt. They had strong self-discipline.

Self-discipline is like your body: The more you train it, the stronger it becomes; the less you train it, the weaker it becomes.

You need to put in the time where it's needed. A lot of excuses are made when we fail, and it is because we refuse to put in the time to do what needs to be done, and to do it correctly.

Sometimes you'll feel motivated, sometimes you won't. But it's not your motivation that will give you the results, it's your actions (practice).

Keep practicing even when you don't feel motivated to do so, and you will start to see the results.

What will make you great will be constantly "working your butt off," regardless of how you feel on any day.

You press on even when you feel like quitting.

If you're growing at all as a ballplayer, then you're going to be a different player next year than you were the year before.

And if you are always pushing yourself to get to the next level, then the changes will often be obvious and fast.

You could be unstoppable. Imagine what you could accomplish if you could simply get yourself to follow through with every practice no matter what!

If you have strong persistence and a consistently great attitude, along with the determination to keep moving toward your goal no matter what obstacles get in the way, you will reach your goals.

CHANGE THE WAY YOU EAT...FOREVER!

While everyone else is eating dessert, go do some pushups.

If you want to play better, live better, breathe easier, and just live a cleaner life, you are going to need to change the typical American eating habits you may have.

Below are some disturbing findings from 2011 that illustrate how unhealthy we Americans are:

1   A large percentage of Americans are considered obese (that is, 20% above their ideal weight). In nine states the obesity rate tops 30%.

2   Americans eat way to much meat—up to 220 pounds per year for every man, woman, and child, and only 14% of Americans consume their daily recommended five servings of fruits and vegetables per day. Our processed food is dense with salt and swimming in high-fructose corn syrup, two flavors Americans can't resist.

3   Currently, food is manufactured in the US as if every American consumes 3,800 calories per day—We only need 2,350 or fewer in a healthy diet

4   A multi-center study showed that American girls as young as seven are entering puberty at DOUBLE the rate they were in the late 1990s, perhaps as a result of the obesity epidemic, but perhaps, too, as a result of the hormones in their environment—including their food.

So, what is it I am recommending you do? Here are a few tips to help you along your path to a healthier diet plan:

1   When at the grocery store, focus mostly on the outer aisles as much as possible. This is where you are going to find the whole and fresh foods. Foods such as real fruits, vegetables, grains, and nuts. Buy these, and find good ways to cook them and make them taste good.

2   Stay away from high-fructose corn syrup. This is typically found in Gatorade, sodas, energy drinks, and, believe it or not, white bread! Read the label on the food you eat, and if you see the suffix "-ose," stay away. Do your best to lay off sugar. All it does is make you fat.

3   If you are having a hard time staying consistent with your diet, write down everything you eat. This is a good way to pay closer attention to what you eat and when, and it will give you an overall view of how much food you consume per day. You may be surprised to see how unhealthy you really are, even if you think you eat healthy.

4   Give up sugar and white anything...white flour, white rice, and white potatoes. These are empty starches with NO nutritional value that just make you hungrier later, thus making you...yes, fat and tired. My preference would be to have you go "brown." Brown rice, quinoa, brown rice pastas. No gluten in these, nothing to weigh you down and make you feel tired. I have found these to be similar tasting and to be a great replacement.

BELIEFS AREN'T REAL

A belief is an acceptance by the mind that something is true or real.

It is often backed up by an emotional or spiritual sense of certainty. We have a high need as humans to prove ourselves right...

Even if we aren't!

Early in life we go out and look for "indications" that will prove that we are right. After we get enough "indications," it becomes a belief.

So in actuality, a belief is not actually true. A belief is just a belief.

So: if your beliefs drive your behavior, which they do, and if your beliefs create a fact in your brain, then you can believe whatever you want to believe.

Fiction can become fact.

How many times have you met a person, and they have a very strong belief in something, and you take a look at it and say to yourself, "I don't know about that!"?

But still they believe it. If they believe it, is that going to drive their behavior?

Yes it will!

If it affects their behavior, is that going to impact and drive their results?

Yes it will.

Here is my point: if you can believe anything you want to believe, you might as well choose something that is going to make you a better ballplayer.

Choose to believe something that will make you a better person. Believe in something that works for you.

Decide to believe in something that is going to move you in the direction you want to go. Believe in something that will get you to the next level.

You determine your future.

Take a look at your beliefs.

Do you believe you are the best player on your team? Do you believe you can do what it takes to get where you need to go? Do you believe in yourself and your talents?

Dig deep and find your beliefs, because they are buried deep inside your brain. Most of us aren't fully aware of what our beliefs really are.

So what you need to ask yourself is this: "What do I have to believe in order to feel and act the way I want to be feeling and acting? What do I need to believe in order to put myself where it is that I want to be?"

What do you need to believe in order to move in the right direction?

These questions may force you to believe in some things that are not absolutely true.

But, again, who is to say what beliefs are true, and what beliefs are not true?

Nobody can, because beliefs aren't true. They are just beliefs.

Take a look at your beliefs, and ask yourself, "What do I NEED to believe in order get myself where I want to go?"

Then, believe it.

DISTRACTIONS WILL KEEP YOU FROM YOUR GOALS

Everyday situations and expectations will present opportunities to us all.

The players who can separate the good from the bad and take advantage of the circumstance at hand will come out ahead.

A lot of ballplayers spend a lot of time and energy focusing on negative circumstances such as field conditions, the fans in the stands, the weather, the other team, or even their coaches.

There is nothing we can do about these situations, and since there is nothing we can do, we need to stop dwelling on them.

Our focus needs to be more on what we can do better to have a better game.

You have got to understand that the fields, the umpire, the weather, the fans—these are all outside factors that should not affect us. Our focus needs to be on ourselves, and not on these other things.

That includes how other people react to how you play.

If you are constantly worrying about playing well for coaches, family, scouts, and friends, then that means you are not attentive to the task at hand.

You don't need to worry about the other team. You don't need to be worried about the fans. You don't need to be worried about all these distractions.

When a spider spins its web, it is not concerned with anything but what comes into its web. And if the spider gets what it wants, what does it do? It attacks its prey. Because that is the only thing that matters.

All you need to worry about is yourself.

****

What outside factors are you concerned with? How will you deal with issues that are "out of your web"? How will you do a better job of controlling things that are in your control?

THE DISCIPLINE TO PURSUE YOUR GOALS

Discipline not only allows you to be in charge of the problems and distractions that will come up in almost every game you play, it also allows you to brush them off easier than other players.

By being disciplined, and demanding that we confront problems, make sacrifices, and challenge our lazy patterns of behavior, we force ourselves to attack some uncomfortable or painful situation.

That is when the lazy ballplayer takes the easy way out and breaks his discipline.

And that is when you are going to shine, because you are a disciplined player.

Most players look for pleasure in order to avoid pain. Going after your problems or taking on difficult situations head on will make you stronger, more self-confident, and much more capable than the next person.

The discipline to be a better player should make you want more problems, and look at them as opportunities to better yourself. It is a twist in thinking we naturally do not embrace.

Most will hope that the problems will simply go away on their own. But the avoidance of problems becomes more painful than the problems themselves, and when the time comes for it all to be said and done, most people will fail.

Discipline is self-control.

Discipline is going after what you want at all costs. Discipline is confronting problems.

It requires strength and character.

Laziness is having a lack of character.

It is getting away with doing as little as possible to get an end result. Laziness has no goals. Laziness is taking the easy way out.

It is delaying what you know you should be doing to the later part of the day. It is avoiding a difficult situation because you are afraid you will fail.

The bottom line; laziness never gets the job done.

Laziness is a learned behavior. That means it can be un-learned.

Discipline takes time and effort, and it forges the will to confront problems that are painful and difficult. The rewards are awesome.

Not only will discipline help you remove the stress caused by the problems, but you will gain inner strength and a feeling of satisfaction knowing that you chose discipline over laziness.

When you recognize it, you will start to welcome difficult situations that you once saw as impossible.

Here is how you will start thinking:

You will not worry, doubt, or question a tough situation. You will now have instinct built up from your hard work, and you will not have to think as hard the next time.

You will trust in yourself, and you will be successful. You will not question your practice or your game. You will trust your instincts. You will find yourself going through extraordinary measures without pain or discomfort.

You will challenge your old thoughts and you will go beyond where you thought you could never go before.

All of this will happen because of your extraordinary commitment to sticking with your goals. You will continue to do well on a regular basis. Nothing that happens in your life will keep you from sticking with your commitment and discipline.

There will be no compromise, you will not take the easy way out, and you will do the right thing every day.

You will do all of this because you believed in yourself from the start, went through the pain to stick to it, and took pride in the fact that you are who you wanted to be.

You motivated yourself the entire time, and you proved to yourself how strong you really are.

Now THAT'S discipline!

****

What small disciplines do you need to work on to improve your game? Are they more mental or physical?

SPORTS AS NOUNS AND VERBS

What are the differences between nouns and verbs?

This is a simple enough question, right?

Let's look at it in a different perspective than we normally do. Let's look at a noun as a solid entity, being, or thing. It is static or fixed.

Let's look at a verb as a process, a routine, or a method we use.

Our use of the two types of words is going to cause a lot of mental slumps and force us to have negative thoughts and we don't even know it!

I will give you an example.

What we tend to do is take some of our processes, routines, and practices and turn them into THINGS. Here is something you may have said in the past: "I did not play well during that game."

Is the GAME a thing?

Or is the game a process?

This is how the Merriam-Webster Dictionary defines "game":

> game
> *noun* \ˈgām\
> **1**
> **a** (1) **:** activity engaged in for diversion or

amusement : play (2) : the equipment for a game
b : often derisive or mocking jesting : fun, sport
<make *game* of a nervous player>
2
a (1) : animals under pursuit or taken in hunting;
especially : wild animals hunted for sport or food
(2) : the flesh of game animals **b** *archaic* : pluck
c : a target or object especially of ridicule or
attack

There is no such thing as a game!

It has a label, and we look at the process of a game as a "thing," but it does not exist anywhere else but in our mind.

Think about this for a minute!

We don't have games! (Huh???)

We have the ACT of playing during a game, and the PROCESS of playing during the game. And a PROCESS is something that changes, and always will.

Here is a different example. Let's take the word "responsibility." Responsibility is a thing.

Or is it really?

There is no such thing as responsibility, but there is such a thing as the ability to respond.

Now it is a process.

When we turn it into a thing, it becomes static in time, as does the idea of a "game."

We have the ability to respond to a situation in THIS moment, and tomorrow I have the ability to respond, and the next day I have the ability to respond, and so on.

Again, think about this. Your parents think of you as a noun.

They look at you, and think of you basically as the person they saw grow up from a baby, and then an adolescent, and then a teenager, and then an adult.

But YOU are a process. You are not a noun. You are not a thing.

You are a PROCESS.

Wrap your brain around this!

You are going to be different tomorrow than you were today.

All of us are like this. Our body is constantly changing.

Look at a picture of yourself five years ago, ten years ago. You will see the changes.

We view the world as a group of nouns.

We objectify everything and turn them into things. We use nouns, label them, freeze them in time, and we see differences rather than association.

Start looking at everything as a process.

All things are a process.

Add an "-ing" to everything when you are done saying it.

Hitting, fielding, reading, driving, "computer-ing."

If you look at everything as a verb rather than a noun, your world will shift and you will see things as shifting.

You will not see things as static and distant from yourself. You will see more similarities and fewer differences.

You may see unification rather than division in your own personal growth.

And maybe you will appreciate some of the little things around you a bit more.

YOU CAN'T UN-RING A BELL

To most people, "someday" means "never."

Virtually everybody we know has the same problem.
They know what is good for them, but they too often
don't do it.

They know they should eat healthier and work out more,
but still don't make beneficial choices. They know they
need to spend their time and money more effectively, but
still fail to do so.

They are always putting others first, while neglecting
their own personal dreams and needs.

What does all of this cause?

It causes us to not get enough sleep and our endless to-do
list to get overlooked day after day. We see it in our
grandparents, our parents, our friends, and in our friends'
parents.

The dream is gone.

If we were to take the time to ask our parents about some
of their dreams they had when they were younger, what
would their reply be? Was their lifelong dream to be
where they are now? Or did it take a different path?

I am constantly seeing that we don't do the things we
know are good for us because we are so busy taking care
of others.

You can't un-ring a bell.

We get so caught up in the day-to-day tasks of going to work, paying the bills, and raising the kids (the lifelong career) that we neglect ourselves.

The dreams become lost.

They fade away into the back of our minds. And while they are in the back of our minds, they can fester and turn into regret.

That regret can turn into blaming others for not reaching our dreams. The blame can become visible and show itself in tense relationships.

And then it's Tuesday. We have to get up again, go to work, pay the bills, and continue the cycle.

This doesn't happen because we don't have enough information on time management or relationship management.
There are plenty of books out there that will teach you how to manage your time.

The problem is how we prioritize our lives and our day-to-day tasks and events.

There are two kinds of people.

The first kind is like most of us. We are more concerned with our responsibilities and how our day-to-day actions affect other people. We are responsible for more than just ourselves, and in order to "help" the people who count on us the most, we will put our own personal matters to the side.

We call ourselves selfless or unselfish.

Our primary focus or motivation is on others and how we help the people we care about. This is our "new" dream. A "selfless" dream.

The second kind of person has different motivations.

Their personal choices are prioritized selfishly.

"What's in it for me?" they ask when considering how to spend their time and energy.

Their own self-interest ranks very high on their list of priorities.

We call these people "selfish."

Their focus is on themselves, their dreams. And who do you think they care and think about the most? Their day-to-day decisions are driven by one force: their own fulfillment.

Think about how someone would describe you.

Maybe you fall right in between the two personality types mentioned above. Maybe you are extreme on one end of the spectrum.

Regardless of where you lie, I feel it is impossible to reach your goals and turn the "Someday" into "Today" if you do not prioritize your own fulfillment at some point and time in your life.

If you wait around until everyone else is taken care of, you will never get around to taking care of yourself.

You won't have anything left to give. And despite how

important we are as individuals, a very tiny portion of the people we all know take the time to prioritize themselves and their dreams.

From this moment on, I want you to commit to prioritizing yourself. But not every minute of every day. Maybe just for thirty minutes per day, or per week.

But DO it!

Take care of yourself.

Love yourself enough that you can trust that there will be more left over for everybody else. Maybe you will be surprised that, somehow, regardless of your busy schedule, you actually feel much better.

This will cause tiny adjustments in your day-to-day habits. You will start to make some new choices.

By taking care of you, you DO take care of others. As a more fulfilled person, you are more fit to engage with and truly help people.

You will see that your refusal to care of yourself actually was not helping you take care of others.

And you will see how the crazy worry you had before was unnecessary the entire time. You will be more confident.

This is going to make you more disciplined.

You will be a more imaginative person, and you will create thoughts and feeling you never knew you were capable of.

It is very important to understand that others won't

necessarily stop taking care of you just because you choose to take some "me" time every once in awhile.

The trick is to believe and trust that your new thought process will work in both directions, and when you feel good, and love yourself first, everything else should fall into place.

****

After reading this chapter, are you more selfish, or unselfish? How often do you put your own thoughts and feelings first? What can you do to take care of yourself more? How will this help you get to your next level?

WHAT WOULD YOU DO IF YOU COULDN'T FAIL?

I'm willing to bet you have heard this before.

How differently would you approach your day or your practice if you knew you could not fail?

What different things would you try if you knew you could not fail?

Fear of change and failure are the biggest hurdles most athletes face when looking to improve their performance.

The kind of success you will see in your future as an athlete is going to depend on how big your vision for your future is.

Do you see yourself playing at the same level, an improved level, or at the top level in the next couple of years?

Take a second and really think about what kind of opportunities are out there.

Think about Division I Universities, or D-II and D-III, or even a powerhouse Junior College. Think about the professional level. Start to visualize the exact place or school you want to see yourself playing at. Close your eyes, and visualize the field, or stadium.

What does the grass or court feel like?

What type of new gear are you playing with? Think about the size of the crowd and how loud it is during a game or match. Really feel how your uniform touches your body.

Who are your teammates? What is your future coach saying to inspire and pump up the team before a big game?

Again, I ask the question, "What would you do differently if you knew you could not fail?"

How differently would you treat today? Are you really giving 100% of your mental and physical talents every single day? And when the little devil on your shoulder starts to creep into your mind and tell you things aren't possible, you have to fight him.

Bury him deep into the back of your brain where he or she belongs. Change the inner conversation you are having with yourself. "I am going to find a way to get to _____ College or University." Or "I am going to find a way to make this season my best ever."

You need to do the things that others around you are not doing. You need to work harder, longer, and smarter than your competition.

It doesn't matter if we are talking about on the field, on the court, in the classroom, or at your job. If you want to be #1, you have to act like it. If becoming #1 came to you easy at this level, you can guarantee it will be tougher at the next level up.

So go out today, and beat your competition somehow. Do ten extra reps, run five more sprints, or stay in the gym twenty minutes longer.

Make this a habit every single day, and watch your vision for your future begin to take shape.

OVERCOME YOUR OBSTACLES

There are a lot of athletes that we all know who face challenges and obstacles every single day. And if you do not think you have obstacles or challenges to overcome, then that should prove you are not pushing yourself.

Sometimes we all fall into a trap of thinking that in order for us to get better we must overcome all of our obstacles and challenges.

And this is true to a certain extent.

We will have to overcome them. But it isn't so much overcoming our problems that make us great at our game.

Anybody who has done anything great in the sports world has had to overcome great obstacles and win many challenges to get where they are. The question is, how? How do we do what the great ones have?

Well, to start, we must accept that through our careers, we are going to face challenges on a regular basis.

They will never stop.

Obstacles are what keep our blood pumping and our desires hot for our sport. So first, let's accept them.

Accept the fact that we are going to encounter them over and over again. That is how sports are. There is no secret recipe or magic wand we can wave to make them disappear.

The reason we must first do this is because denying them

can cause them to get bigger.

Turning away from them and not addressing challenges with a positive outlook and a willingness to improve will make it blow up in your face.

It is like throwing a gasoline tank into a dumpster fire. You won't make the fire any smaller, you are going to make it bigger!

We see it time and time again when an athlete is in denial about what they are about to face, or in denial about the obstacles they must beat in order to get better. Everyone else can see it—the fans, coaches, other players—but the guy or girl with the problem just can't see it.

They are unwilling to listen, or accept it.

Of course, this is much easier said than done. Take a moment to think about what you are fighting in your game right now.

Whatever it may be that you are refusing to accept is going to refuse to go away. It will linger on and continue to stay with you until you address it.

The minute you stop denying it will be the moment you begin to develop and improve it. It will make your advancement a whole lot easier.

We have to accept and embrace our struggles, challenges, obstacles, problems—whatever you want to call them—and utilize them to our advantage.

Recognize your hurdles, and you will find a way to jump over them.

TODAYS DECISIONS AFFECT TOMORROW

This concept seems simple enough, right?

What happens today is a direct reflection of the decisions that I made yesterday and the days before. Practicing extra, running farther, or studying harder.

Can you accept responsibility for your actions and accept the fact that you are in control of your own life?

Do you believe that your actions drive your life, or do outside conditions shape it?

In sports, we can look back on game-time situations and decisions and realize it is not what happened in the game that we remember, it is our emotional reactions to the events that stick in our brain.

Think about an exciting game or moment within one, like watching someone winning a championship.

What is it that sticks out?

In most cases we will remember the emotional response. And this ties in with the old saying we all have heard before: "It is not what happens to you that defines who you are, it is how you react that defines you."

Our true character will come out in times of adversity.

How did we act when the pressure was on? Did we fold? Did we back down?

Or did we stand up like we know we should, and inspire our teammates to battle?

It is in our makeup to take action or control, not to be controlled or allow things to happen to us.

You wouldn't be reading this right now if you didn't allow "things" and "stuff" to control your life. And when I say "take action and control," I am not telling you to be unbearable and difficult to be around.

I am simply saying you need to see that it is your duty to make things happen. Do it! Be a leader. Show your teammates how it is done.

Inspire others.

Over the years, I have come across many people who have wanted to put themselves in a better position in life, or in their sport, or wanted to push through to the next level. They wanted to show the world that they could do it!

So we talk about a plan, and we put together an arrangement with the proper intentions prepped out, and both of us have a good understanding of what we both need to do.

But then something happens. Somebody forgot, or did not take the steps needed to make it work.

And the response is usually the same.

They lost the steam they had in the beginning, and "stuff" got in the way. Essentially, they were waiting for something to happen to them, or they were waiting for someone to help them.

There is no initiative.

If we take the time to look around us and see who is out there making things happen, we will notice it is the action-takers, the players with the most initiative, and the athletes with the best plan who are the ones we look up to.

You are responsible for your own future. You need to take action and responsibility if you want something to turn out the way you intend.

What attitude will you approach today with?

We have two choices.

> 1. Get out there and make something happen.
> Or
> 2. Sit back and wait for something to happen to us.

The responsibility is yours. The opportunities are out there.

If you do not take control of your own feelings and actions...prepare to suffer the consequences: a life filled with regret.

EVERYTHING MUST COME FROM WITHIN YOU

Understand that you are the cause of everything that happens to you. Understand that you are either making things happen or not making things happen.

My example here will be college recruitment.

Recruitment for college doesn't randomly happen for you. You have to commit to it 100% or you will not get 100% back in return.

You must be clear about where you want to go to college. Start with a long list, and work your way through it until the choices are apparent.

The more details you put into your plan to get to the school of your choice, the more likely the groundwork is laid to get you there. Your approach must be relentless, and the action you take towards the school must be purposeful.

You will not reach the desired outcome unless you act with purpose!

You cannot just fantasize of going to the school of your dreams, you must do something about it!

You see, many athletes say that they have very strong interest in getting to the school of their dreams.

But as we meet more and more of them, we notice that very few have actually done it!

The problem is, about 95% of all athletes who claim they want to go to a fantastic university don't take the proper steps or follow the right plan.

That leaves 5% of athletes who actually achieve their goal.

Why does this happen?

It isn't about luck. The 5% took action!

They actually did something! They did not sit around and wait for someone to do it for them.

Being proactive and taking initiative is what we all know we need to do in all aspects of our lives.

Yet we fail at it time and time again.

Today is the day to break that habit!

Do something about it today! It doesn't even have to be something big.

It can be something as small as writing a letter and putting it in the mail. If you don't have the money for postage, write an email.

It is free!

And if you are beyond college and this example is too youthful for you, change the example to job searching, or asking a girl out on a date, or starting a business.

If we do not take greater accountability for our actions, we cannot expect to grow and receive great results.

KEEP YOUR EYES OPEN

As a young recruit, day in and day out, you have got to keep your nose to the grindstone.

You know why?

Because every single year, thousands of coaches have to set out and find the next set of capable athletes to come in and fill the spots of seniors that are leaving their programs.

Every year, thousands of coaches award over one billion dollars in athletic scholarships.

Don't let an opportunity like this slip through your fingers. If you sit back and wait for an offer, it is likely that it won't be headed your way.

A journey of a thousand miles begins with the first step.

The earlier you start the better.

Be proactive, and take action with your recruitment! There is no better time than today.

BRING ON THE SETBACKS!

The question isn't if we will or will not hit disappointments, struggles, adversity, or setbacks.

Because we will.

The question is how we will react to them? How are you going to personally deal with them? Are you going to be like everyone else and stress over it? Will it ruin your day? Are you going to let the negativity carry over into tomorrow?

Well, many people do exactly that!

They get upset. They become hopeless and frustrated. They trash talk the "other guy" and point the finger rather than accept responsibility and take some form of accountability for the setbacks they face. I suggest we attempt to take a more positive approach.

If we take some time and look back in hindsight, we will find out the little problems or bumps in the road were not as significant as we had previously thought. You can even look at them as an important part of BECOMING a successful athlete.

The good moments wouldn't feel as good if we never had the sad, gut-wrenching pain of loss. When I look back in life and think of the hard times, regretful moments, and painful struggles, I realize that had I not been through them, I would not be in the place that I am now. I would not have the wonderful relationships I have.

I may have missed out on some fantastic moments. And most importantly, I never would have had the chance to LEARN from my life.

The thing—or trick is—to use not only our past events but our current ones as well to move on. Live for tomorrow rather than living today and thinking about yesterday. Dwelling on a setback or sulking in our negative juices isn't going to make us better athletes, coaches, or people.

Let's use those juices to make the necessary adjustments and move ahead. This can be a powerful way to feel better about ourselves in the moment, far better than living with self-deprecating stress or criticism that spreads to our teammates, friends, and family.

Get up, work harder, boost up your mental energy, and release the pressure and frustration from your shoulders.

Today is a new day. Let's make it the best we can.

TAKE WHAT IS OFFERED TO YOU

In general, athletes don't always take advice.

Even good advice from knowledgeable coaches.

Even when it is offered from a kind heart.

Even when it is offered for free.

Think about some of the times in your life when you have been offered some advice. How often do you take someone else's advice and apply it?

When was the last time someone told you something to help you out and you said, "Hey! That's a good idea, I'm going to try it!" or "I never thought of doing it like that, I like it, let's do it!" It is very rare to hear that from a lot of athletes today.

They want to do the same things they have been doing, regardless of the success level they have reached.

If you are doing the same things over and over and not getting the results you want, what do you think the problem is? Sometimes in order to get better as an athlete you need to view things differently.

You need to make adjustments. You need to open your eyes to see opportunities that are in front of your face.

How can you see something in front of your face if your eyes and ears are closed to suggestions from other people?

Why do we do this, you may be asking?

Well, maybe the reason is we are just hard headed, or stubborn.

We want to do things our own way regardless of the results we are getting now. What worked for us in the past will NOT ALWAYS work for us in the present. We have to make adjustments, right?

Maybe the reason is fear. Maybe we are worried we will look bad in the eyes of our teammates, parents, fans, or worse yet, a scout watching a game! We never want to look incompetent, right?

What if the opinion given won't help? Is your ego saying, "If I can't figure it out, how is this person supposed to know what to do?"

Perhaps we took some instruction and it backfired on us in the past. That type of thing happens all the time.

Here is what I think. Take what is being said, try it, use it, apply it, and test your results. Your game can be so much easier if you absorb what is being said and soak it up into your brain. Use what other athletes have done before you and make it one of the strengths of your game.

Because if you already knew everything, you would be doing it already, right?

The bottom line is, if you are struggling, you need advice. Take it. It will make your life easier. Especially if the advice is coming from someone who has been in your shoes at one point in time.

Many athletes have missed out on so many opportunities just because they didn't apply the advice they were given. I have seen it over and over.

The kid was just a step away or was headed on the right path but came up just shy of reaching his goal. If he would have just listened and done what was given to him, he would have made it. If only he had opened his eyes!

This is just a small, mental adjustment we can make to improve ourselves as athletes and people in general. Don't let a minor thing like stubbornness get in your way. There is tons of advice out there. Seek it out. People are willing to help you. Open your mind to new suggestions. Open your mind to other opinions.

Listen. And learn to pay attention.

It may be the hurdle you have been trying to jump over to get you where you want to be.

CHARACTER IS EVERYTHING!

What does character have to do with playing sports at the collegiate level? It isn't going to make you run faster, lift more weights, or be more powerful at your position. So, "What does it have to do with me, and what does it have to do with sports?", you may be asking.

Well, the answer is: everything!

It means everything for a couple of reasons.

First, it shows others that you do things the right way. You have a solid conscience. As you move away from home, you are going to see temptations coming at you from every angle. Peer pressure will increase, and your morals will be tested on a regular basis.

Second, character shows you stand up for what you believe in and speak up for what you feel is wrong. You are a leader, and you let others around you know when you see something inappropriate. You have courage.

A coach is not going to have to worry about you following a crowd or choosing temporary satisfaction over long-term results. They won't have to worry about you breaking the rules. Your coach will not worry about you disrespecting the community and embarrassing the team and what the team represents.

You are accountable, and you accept responsibility for your actions. This is what character has to do with being an athlete at the college level.

Remember this as you go through your career. Remember your roots and what got you where you are today. If you stick with the same principles we all have learned at a young age you can't go wrong.

Be courageous, be a leader, and be loyal to those who have sacrificed so hard for your future.

Character is everything.

SNAP OUT OF IT!

I have found that most athletes really believe that they have no control over their emotions. They think that the way things happen to them is just by drifting through what they are doing, reacting to things that happen to them, and then floating along with the rest of the tide.

Just keep doing what everyone else is doing, right? Taking advice from people who have never done it before, allowing them to tell you what "should" have been done.

They live life in hindsight.

They are hyper-critical of people or coaches. They let you know what "they would have done" if they were in charge. They talk a big game, but have very little game to show for it. I bet you know someone like this now. I bet you can say this person's name out loud right now! I bet the thought of some of the stupid things they have said is driving you up the wall!

Snap out of it.

You actually have complete and total control over your emotional state. Don't let that person control your emotions. You have full control over your brain. Full control ranging from the positive thoughts all the way to the adrenaline plunks.

My goal is to force athletes to realize what is going on. That way they don't get fooled. They don't believe every myth and meme they come across. That way they understand that there are many, many ways to get to the next level. Physically, emotionally, and academically: as an athlete you have to win in all of those categories. Two out of three ain't bad, but it won't cut the mustard. We need three for three.

You need to be a hammer! A hammer pounds nails into wood, or it can be used to pound holes in a wall. The dang tool won't care what you do with it; it's just a tool.

Utilize the crazy people you meet, the stuff you read, and resources you have as TOOLS to help get you to the next level.

Don't react to your life as it happens to you. Control what happens inside that brain of yours, and start looking very hard at how YOU and the CRAZIES deal with things that happen to them.

Understand that everyone is scared. The best athletes can recognize that fear. They push it off the table, pull up their socks, and get down to business.

Snap out of it! We have too much to do. Let's get to it!

WHAT WILL YOU CONTRIBUTE?

Are you going to be missed when you are gone?

The same person who put you in your current position is the same person who can get you where you want to go.

That person is you.

If you have a map to a treasure chest, follow it. Once you open the treasure, you will find more maps to more treasure.

Do you want to leave a legacy? How much will you contribute to society?

How can you make today the best day of your life?

You need to have a big reason WHY you want to be where you want to be!

Fully associate yourself with your outcome. Get specific with what you want in life.

Real regret only comes from not doing your best.

Do more than is expected of you. It will be less likely you live with regret.

Every moment is another chance to turn it around.

At some point in time in your life, you are going to get knocked down. At some point, you are going to get your teeth kicked in. You will have some bad days. You aren't going to go three for three or four for four every game.

And everybody loves a success story. But what is more interesting and more inspirational is a comeback story. Over life's long journey, being relentless toward what you want is probably the best characteristic you can possess. How resilient are you?

Life has a funny way of becoming easier when you work hard and becoming hard when you live easy. How well can you take a punch? How quickly do you recover from it? How do you handle criticism?

A lot of us wonder why we do not get as much accomplished as we could.

It is because of our resilience.

GO FOR IT!

If you are going to do something that is important, the best time to start is now. The best time is not later on in the day, or tomorrow, next week, or next month. Change your mindset and have a "go for it" attitude.

We can always find a reason or an excuse to put something off. And I will bet it's a pretty good reason. But behind that pretty good reason is usually just plain old fear or laziness.

We may not be lazy or fearful with every other thing in our lives...just the thing we keep putting off.

So I don't care if you think you have a good excuse. Ignore it and go for it now! Athletes who dive in and are more aggressive enjoy a much higher level of success than those who wait. Their mindset is more engaged in what they are doing, and because they are successful, they are having more fun.

I spoke to an athlete about improving his footwork and speed. The first thing I said was, "If you want to get faster, you need to work at it." I told him it would not happen unless he put the work in every single day. We talked about sprints, form, and repetition.

A couple of weeks passed, and we had an opportunity to see each other again. Sure enough, he'd put no extra work or effort into his speed game. No extra reps, no agility work. There were definitely excuses as to why he couldn't put in the work—schoolwork, family events, and forgetfulness.

Despite all of these reasons, I explained how we all have a lot of "stuff" going on in our lives. Waiting and finding just the right time isn't going to get it done. You gotta "go for it!"

The key to your success may be simply understanding that no matter what the obstacles and responsibilities are, the best time to start is today.

I'm not saying you should do absolutely everything all in one day, but you do need to get started. Just getting going, for most people, is the hard part, not the task of continually putting it off.

Once you finally go for it, everything else will start to fall into place.

So again, go for it! If you truly commit to something, and put in the time, I'm willing to bet you will feel the changes you are looking to find.

LET THE HATERS HATE

In the world we live in, if you start to do something significant, or if you have a strong opinion about something, people will begin to hate on you. They will have bad things to say about your message, and you will find that you will probably make enemies just as easily as you make friends.

What you need to do is understand why people act like this. If you understand why, you won't have a problem when you find out that there are people out there who don't agree with you. You will not get discouraged from your goals because you feel you are a bad person or feel there is something wrong with you.

Here is how I think you should look at the situation should it happen to you.

Realize that if someone feels this way toward you, it means you made an impact in their life. The odd are, though, that what you stand for is a threat to their daily habits. Basically, your persona represents an idea they wish they could live up to. So, odds are, you are a threat to their happiness, their confidence, or their goals.

Do not blame the hater directly for their behavior or opinion. If you do this you will actually make your own life more difficult. Whenever you hear of these situations, blame the circumstances that person may be living with, and instead realize it is their problem or issue, not yours.

Take what the haters say or feel, and use it to fuel your desire to win.

If at some point you think you will lose your mind because you hear negative feedback about you, then you should control yourself instead of displaying how frustrated you are.

Here is the thing: the people who don't have confidence in themselves hate their rivals and competitors. These people hate on you because of their own mental weaknesses. Your sanity will actually depend on how well you can handle the people who don't agree with your opinions and how you act.

The best way for you to feel is to pity them.

Because if they don't get on the steamroller you are driving, they will get run over.

THE LIGHTS WONT TURN ON UNTILL...

"Do what you should do, when you should do it, whether you feel like it or not."—Thomas Huxley

How many hours have you practiced this week? How many hours have you practiced on your own, without a coach or parent pushing you?

The things you do when nobody is looking are the skills that separate the good from the great.

Great players have an agenda.

If you are focused, you have an agenda. And your agenda is what you are planning to achieve in both the short term and over the long run.

It means visualizing your future so that the "plan" you created becomes closer to a reality.

What does it take to beat your competition?

Drive.

I cannot stress enough the importance of self-discipline. And self-discipline is directly linked with motivation.

What are your motives? What drives you? What is it you really want?

Why are you playing your sport? Are you just playing for fun? Were you pushed into it by your parents? Is it a love for the game? Do you see yourself at the next level? Do you see yourself playing successfully there?

I do not think you would be reading this if your parents forced you to do something. I do not think you would be reading this if your only reason for playing was for fun.

That is a huge part of it, having fun, but something else has to be there.

I think the best word to describe that feeling is passion. If you do not have passion for something, it is likely you won't be very good at it.

Hitting the switch is not something you do physically, but mentally. Self-discipline, motivation, and passion are all keys to success.

The more passion you feel, the more motivated you will be. The more motivated you are, the more self-disciplined you will be.

If you are self-disciplined, you will put in the hard work it takes to be a success. When you put in the work, you are taking control of your situation.

You are taking control of your life, and you are going to be more confident because you know you are moving closer to your goals.

Self-discipline is the key to athletic greatness.

It is the quality that opens all opportunities for you and makes the impossible possible. With self-discipline, the average player can get places farther and faster than their talents and intelligence can.

But without self-discipline, a talented player with every

God-given ability or blessed circumstance will rarely rise above mediocrity. Unfortunately, this happens far too often.

Don't let it happen to you.

****

FOOD FOR YOUR THOUGHTS

1. What is the most important characteristic or trait a leader has?

2. What attribute do you feel is most responsible for the success you have now?

3. Was there a turning point in your life when the "light switch" was turned on?

4. What do you think is the best way a player can maintain or sustain success?

5. What do you do differently than other people?

6. If you could change anything, what would it be?

7. What is the last thought that goes through your mind when you go to sleep at night?

8. If you only had one month get something accomplished, what would you do? What people would you make sure you spoke to?

9. What do you think are the qualities that separate elite athletes (or leaders) from average athletes (or people)?

10. How do you think Facebook/Twitter/YouTube is changing our culture and shaping our youth?